# IMAGES
## OF THE
## WAFFEN-SS

*Also by Mark Yerger*
SS-STURMBANNFÜHRER ERNST AUGUST KRAG
RIDING EAST: THE SS CAVALRY BRIGADE IN POLAND AND RUSSIA 1939-1942

# IMAGES OF THE WAFFEN-SS

## A PHOTO CHRONICLE OF GERMANY'S ELITE TROOPS

### MARK C. YERGER

**Schiffer Military History**
Atglen, PA

## ACKNOWLEDGMENTS

My thanks goes to literally hundreds of people who have helped in every way possible. The following are among those who assisted in this album as well as past volumes:

Otto Baum
Gerd Bremer
Hermann Buch
Hans Kempin
Karl Kreutz
Ernst August Krag
Kurt Imhoff
Josef Lainer
Fritz Langanke
Jakob Lobmeyer
James Lucas
Jess Lukens
Otto Kumm
John Moore
Zuzana Pivcova
Ortwin Pohl
Ruth Sommers
Jost Schneider
Otto Weidinger

### DEDICATION
*To the collectors, historians and friends who have
helped me through the years*

Book Design by Robert Biondi.

Printed in the United States of America.
ISBN: 0-7643-0078-4

We are interested in hearing from authors with book ideas on related topics.

Published by Schiffer Publishing Ltd.
77 Lower Valley Road
Atglen, PA 19310
Please write for a free catalog.
This book may be purchased from the publisher.
Please include $2.95 postage.
Try your bookstore first.

# CONTENTS

Introduction    6

*Chapter 1*    8
**THE SS OFFICER SCHOOLS
BRAUNSCHWEIG AND BAD TÖLZ**

*Chapter 2*    23
**SS FLAGS AND STANDARDS**

*Chapter 3*    35
**IMAGES OF THE ELITE**

# INTRODUCTION

*This photo book is in response to the readers of my "Knights of Steel" series on the 2.SS-Panzer-Division "Das Reich." Many of them wrote me about their specific interests and wishes regarding more photos from that division and the other classic units "Leibstandarte," "Totenkopf," and "Wiking." This majority of this first album covers these classic divisions though others are included as well.*

*Should I receive sufficient requests from readers, other albums will be planned. Any readers wishing specific topics or individuals for inclusion in future photo books are asked to inform me of their choices by writing to me directly at P.O. Box 4485, Lancaster, PA 17604, USA.*

*The requests I received were not only from unit historians but model builders, armor enthusiasts, autograph and memorabilia collectors, as well as those whose interest are holders of the Knight's Cross. I hope this first album fills a number of wishes expressed by those readers. The photos are this book, so captions have been kept to a minimum to allow largest photo size for best detail.*

*The Waffen-SS field troops were Germany's elite and interest in them continues to grow. These photos are only an addendum to the numerous valuable texts available on many facets of the subject.*

*Mark C. Yerger*
*1996*

# 1

## SS OFFICER SCHOOLS
## BRAUNSCHWEIG
## AND BAD TÖLZ

*The Waffen-SS utilized numerous training facilities created specifically for the SS as well as Army specialized training centers. These training areas encompassed the numerous areas of equipment and occupational specialties needed for a modern military. The SS also had specialized training areas (SS-Truppenübungsplatz) which incorporated several schools and were often used for the formation or refurbishment of entire divisions. The schools and training areas also contained the specialized replacement units used by the divisions. Many of these units fought late in the war as independent battle groups (Kampfgruppen). Schools for training NCOs as well as officers were established. The first SS schools formed were SS officer academies in Braunschweig and Bad Tölz. These were the most influential with regard to the fighting leadership of the Waffen-SS. The list of graduating cadets from the pre-war courses held at these two schools is a veritable "who's who" of battalion, regimental and divisional commanders as well as numerous senior staff officers. Many were awarded the Knight's Cross or German Cross in Gold.*

*The first school established was Bad Tölz in 1934 and the initial class graduated that year. The following year Braunschweig was created. Full length courses (ten months) continued until 1939. In wartime the length of training was shortened and in both cases graduates often attended supplemental specialized courses after graduation. Graduates went to many sections of the SS as well as Police organizations.*

This overall frontal view shows Bad Tölz before the trees existing today grew obscuring the outline.

The entrance to Bad Tölz. The school was specially built for the SS and Paul Lettow served as first school commander. Among the 1934 first course graduates were Fritz Klingenberg (later commander of 17.SS-Panzer-Grenadier-Division "Götz von Berlichingen," holder of the Knight's Cross and German Cross in Gold), Hans Kempin (last commander of the 32.SS-Freiwilligen-Grenadier-Division "30 Januar"), Georg Schönberger (commander Panzer Regiment "Leibstandarte" and Knight's Cross holder) and Martin Stange (last commander of the 38.SS-Panzer-Grenadier-Division "Nibelungen" and awarded the German Cross in Gold).

The archway at the school entrance. Allied commanders thought it the most advanced officer training area they'd ever seen. At the end of the war the final cadet class provided the officer cadre for the 38.SS-Panzer-Grenadier-Division "Nibelungen." This division, the last created by the SS, was first led by the last school commander, SS-Obersturmbannführer Richard Schulz. The school survived the war undamaged and still exists. Among the nine different commanders of the school between 1934-45 was Fritz Klingenberg who graduated from there in 1934.

Rear view of Bad Tölz. The school still exists and was used as a police officer training academy in the 1980s.

Two front views of Braunschweig taken in 1935. Formerly an Army training institution, it was taken over by the SS in 1934 and command given to Paul Hausser. Classes began in 1935 and Hausser later became inspector for both SS officer schools. The building was destroyed by an air raid in 1944 and the facility moved to Posen-Treskau.

A cadet lounge in Braunschweig.

A staircase inside Braunschweig shown in August 1935. Many of the rooms with historical significance were preserved.

The statue on top of SS officer school Braunschweig. The chariot was an observation platform that could be reached from inside the school.

The swimming hall built at Braunschweig shown in late summer 1935.

Cadets and facility made designs in various areas of the grounds from stones during the first class at Braunschweig. The two shown are by a teaching detachment and the other by a teaching group. Note one reproduces the special collar insignia worn by facility and cadets while at the academy.

Reichsführer-SS Heinrich Himmler (right) and other SS dignitaries inspect the Braunschweig cadets on June 30, 1935. Next to Himmler wearing helmet is SS-Standartenführer Paul Hausser (school commander) and left of Hausser is Himmler's adjutant Karl Wolff.

Just as the officer school cadets became wartime combat leaders so did their instructors. Shown here at Braunschweig in 1935 are, right, SS-Oberführer Paul Hausser (commander of "Das Reich", II.SS-Panzer-Korps, and finally in command of an Army Group) being briefed by school instructor SS-Obersturmbannführer Matthias Kleinheisterkamp (commanded "Nord", Das Reich" and "Polizei" divisions and finally VI.SS-Armee-Korps). Both men were highly decorated and attained senior rank. Hausser ended the war as an SS-Oberst-Gruppenführer awarded the Knight's Cross with Oakleaves and Swords. Kleinheisterkamp, also awarded the Swords to the Knight's Cross, ended the war as an SS-Obergruppenführer. Of all his accomplishments Hausser was most proud of Braunschweig.

ABOVE: In June of 1935 the first class of cadets hear a speech by Reichsführer-SS Heinrich Himmler in front of Braunschweig.

OPPOSITE ABOVE: Heinrich Himmler, on the edge of the step, is surrounded by SS, Luftwaffe and Army visitors for the occasion of his speech to the cadets and faculty in June 1935. 2nd from the right is Himmler's adjutant Karl Wolff, then Friedrich Jeckeln (later commander of V.SS-Gebirgs-Korps and Knight's Cross winner) and Walter Schmitt of the SS Main Office (SS-Hauptamt).

OPPOSITE BELOW: The dignitaries in the previous photo salute at the end of the June 1935 ceremony. The first graduate of the SS officer schools to attain general rank was Franz Augsburger. A 1935 class cadet at Braunschweig, he commanded the 20.Waffen-Grenadier-Division der SS (estinische Nr.1) and won the Knight's Cross. Other eventual divisional commanders who attended the first class at Braunschweig were Hans Mühlenkamp ("Wiking" and "30.Januar"), Sylvester Stadler ("Hohenstaufen"), Karl Ullrich ("Wiking"), Hans Lingner ("Götz von Berlichingen") and Otto Baum ("Das Reich", "Götz von Berlichingen" and "Reichsführer-SS"). Rudolf Lehmann (Bad Tölz 1935 class, later "Das Reich" commander) and Hugo Krass (Braunschweig 1937 class, last commander "Hitlerjugend") also were cadets and became divisional commanders. All these men except Augusberger and Lingner won the Oakleaves to the Knight's Cross. Otto Baum and Sylvester Stadler won the Swords.

SS-Untersturmführer Karl Sattler wears his dress black overcoat and sword. He displays the "SS Schule Braunschweig" sleeve stripe. A similar one was worn by personnel attached to Bad Tölz. Sattler served with the SS/VT and Totenkopfverbande before the war and became an SS-Sturmbannführer on June 21, 1944. He won the Knight's Cross on January 16, 1945 in command of a Kampfgruppe after serving as a company commander, adjutant and battalion commander with SS-Panzer-Grenadier-Regiment 21, 10.SS-Panzer-Division "Frundsburg" for most of 1943-44.

Special insignia was worn by cadets and facilty at both schools. Here Willi Hund wears the "JST" monogram on his shoulder board for Bad Tölz. He won the Knight's Cross on May 9, 1945 as an SS-Obersturmführer commanding a Battle Group (Kampfgruppe) of the SS-Panzer-Grenadier-Regiment 23 "Norge." On the right is Gerhard Rothe as a Braunschweig instructor and SS-Untersturmführer.

In addition to shoulder boards and sleeve insignia, a distinctive collar insignia with "B" (for Braunschweig) or "T" (Bad Tölz) was worn. Here the former is displayed by facilty member SS-Hauptsturmführer Hermenegild von Westphalen who won the German Cross in Gold on April 23, 1944 as commander of SS-Panzer-Grenadier-Regiment 24 "Danmark." He taught at the school in 1937 and during 1942-43. On the right is Otto Weidinger.

# 2

## SS FLAGS
## AND STANDARDS

*All military units have had flags or colors designating their particular unit or to be used in various ceremonial occasions and the SS was no exception. The Following photographs give only a sample of the wide variety of patterns used and occasions they were displayed.*

The "Jingling Johnnie" displayed at the head of an SS band was among the most ornate ceremonial trappings. The wide center piece with stylized eagle heads forming its ends was engraved with the name of the unit. As can be seen its weight required a suitably strong NCO to carry it for extended periods. The example shown is from Regiment "Deutschland" with the band leader standing on the left with sword.

A more detailed view of the top and banner of the "Jingling Johnnie" belonging to Regiment "Deutschland."

The impressive decor of an SS mess during the pre-war period displays several SS banners and flags.

Hitler consecrates SS standards at the Nuremberg rally by touching them with the "Blood Flag" that had been carried in the abortive 1923 Putsch. Behind the standard bearer (note bearers neck gorget for SS or SA standard bearers) is Karl Wolff. The man near right wears an early lionhead pattern SS sword with knot. In the background can be seen the square red "Deutschland Erwache" (Germany Awake) regimental standards, one of which was given to each pre-war SS regiment. (Schneider)

Massed SS standards at Nuremberg show the pre-war dress black uniform worn by the SS Verfügungstruppe (Special Purpose Troops) that later became the Waffen-SS. A name plate on the standard displays the regimental title though in the case of some Death's Head Units (SS-Totenkopfverbände) a skull with the Roman numeral designation of the unit was used. Standing in front right is SS-Obersturmbannführer Carl-Maria Demelhuber who ended the war as an SS-Obergruppenführer in command of XVI.SS-Armee-Korps. (Schneider)

A huge black and white death's head flag in front of assembled personnel of SS-Totenkopfstandarte "Oberbayern." As a regiment the unit became part of the "Totenkopf" Division.

A rare view of a Standarte of the SS-Totenkopfverbände, in this instance II./3.SS-Totenkopfstandarte "Thuringen."

Another huge flag, in this case the black SS building type, being flown atop the entrance of SS Training Camp Prittlbach.

Battalion flags were carried by most pre-war units and continued to be displayed in the early war years. An embroidered patch in the upper corner designated the unit. Shown here is the flag of the reconnaissance detachment (Aufklärungsabteilung) of the SS/VT. The patch SSAA shows the abbreviation of of Aufklärungsabteilung: "AA." The unit retained the flaf when it became a component of "Das Reich." On the right marching is SS-Untersturmführer Fritz Vogt, later awarded the Knight's Cross. The men in Panzer uniforms wear the unusual early black beret crash helmet. Other units, such as the engineer and signal battalions carried flags with unit patches incorporating their special pre-war insignia.

The black and white flag with SS runes in front of a Radolfzell barracks.

The battalion flag of II./"Deutschland" in front of the Dachau town hall in 1935 prior to the unit's move to Munich. The patch ID reads II/SS1.

In the later war years it was rare to see large flag displays except for distinguished ceremonies. Here a special area with field guns, battalion flags and SS banners has been set up in Niedermarzbürg in 1944 on the day Regiment "Der Führer" commander Otto Weidinger was awarded the Knight's Cross. Note the SS decorated torches. Weidinger's award, while given when a regimental commander, was actually for his leadership of the reconnaissance detachment of "Das Reich."

SS barracks entrance, 1940.

SS banners, flags and, if available, unit standards were used in Russia only for award ceremonies and funerals. Here services are held in Russia for an officer in the engineer battalion of the SS-Kavallerie-Division.

Although not a flag as such, the most notable cloth materials were the kettle drum covers and trumpet carried by unit bands. Here is an impressive display of the buglers and drummer of SS-Totenkopfstandarte "Oberbayern" during the pre-war years.

Men of "Oberbayern" assembled with SS and Death's Head emblem flags prior to formation of the "Totenkopf" Division.

# 3

## IMAGES OF
## THE ELITE

Pzkpfw III of "Wiking" during its 1942 first deployment of armor.

Shown with a "D" monogrammed shoulder board designating his unit as Regiment "Deutschland," SS-Oberscharführer Walter Hummel was a qualified paratrooper and so was allowed to wear a rarely seen paratroop badge on his SS uniform.

Completely effective camouflage uniforms and helmet covers are worn by these "Leibstandarte" troops. The officer in the foreground is eventual "LAH" regimental commander and Oakleaves winner Albert Frey. Frey wrote his memoirs after the war and they offer valuable insight into the regimental commander's career.

A Pzkpfw III and a camouflaged Pzkpfw 38 (SdKfz 139) anti-tank vehicle of "Wiking" in Russia during the second phase of the Russian campaign.

A Panzer III of "Wiking" carrying extra road wheels attached to its hull in Russia.

Panzer IVs of "Das Reich" showing the Kursk period vehicle marking on the rear fender.

Note the SS runes made of wood at this cemetery entrance, complete with guard of honor. The officer in overseas cap is "Leibstandarte" German Cross and Knight's Cross holder Rudolf Sandig.

Panzer IIIs of "Leibstandarte" in column formation, indicating transport towards the front lines in Russia.

This pair of "Leibstandarte" Panzer IIIs are shown in the autumn of 1943.

A "Das Reich" Panzer IV (note division tactical emblem) in Kharkov during March 1943.

Three Knight's Cross holders of "Wiking" during a celebration in the field. From left are SS-Hauptsturmführer Walter Schmidt (Regiment "Westland," later Oakleaves winner), SS-Obersturmbannführer August Dieckmann (Regiment "Germania," later Swords winner) and SS-Hauptscharführer Albert Müller (Regiment "Westland").

A "Das Reich" staff meeting during the Normandy campaign. From left are Otto Reimann (Anti-aircraft Detachment commander and German Cross holder), Albert Stückler (1st Staff Officer and German Cross holder), Ernst August Krag (Assault Gun Detachment commander and Oakleaves to the Knight's Cross holder), Heinz Lammerding (Divisional Commander and Knight's Cross winner) and Dieter Kesten (Divisional Adjutant and Knight's Cross holder with Panzer Regiment "Das Reich").

A well camouflaged Tiger I (Pzkpfw VI) of "Leibstandarte" in the winter of 1942-43.

Tiger "424" of the "Leibstandarte" during the second Russian winter.

Hans Scherg being awarded the Knight's Cross by the commander of the SS-Polizei-Division, SS-Brigadeführer Fritz Schmedes (note his cufftitle).

In this signed portrait, SS-Unterscharführer Ewald Ehm wears all his decorations including single handed tank destruction strips, his German Cross in Gold awarded on September 16, 1943 and on his sleeve both the "Deutschland" cufftitle and his badge for Engineer Assault Boat Coxswain. He was also awarded the rare Close Combat Clasp in Gold. Ehm served with the 16th Company (engineers) of "Deutschland." At right is Michael Wittmann, top scoring tank ace of the Waffen-SS, being presented with the Swords to the Knight's Cross.

Two views of a Tiger I advancing with engineers of "Das Reich" during the summer of 1943.

A Kursk marked "Tiger" of "Das Reich" during the summer 1943 battles.

Another Kursk period photo of a "Das Reich" Tiger I.

Two Panthers (Pzkpfw V) of "Wiking" in Russia.

"Totenkopf" Knight's Cross holder Fritz Christian with his anti-tank weapon.

**Panther "613" of the "Wiking" Panzer Regiment with side skirts to protect the road wheels from infantry anti-tank weapons.**

**A Panther of II.SS-Panzer-Korps in Germany during 1944.**

Heinrich Hoffmann photographed many Knight's Cross holders and numerous portraits were made into postcards collected by Germany's youth. This signed example of Max Wünsche as an SS-Sturmbannführer with "Leibstandarte" was taken before he won the Oakleaves on August 11, 1944 with "Hitlerjugend."

This pre-war Regiment "Germania" group photo shows early enlisted man's uniforms. Fourth from the right is eventual SS-Regiment "de Ruyter" Knight's Cross holder Karl-Heinz Ertel.

SS-Oberführer Carl-Maria Demelhuber (right) wears the early pattern collar insignia in this 1940 photo when he commanded Regiment "Germania." The men of his unit still wear the "SS2" collar insignia for that regiment as well.

**Panther "612" of Panzer Regiment 5, "Wiking."**

**An Sdkfz 138 of II.SS-Panzer-Korps in the summer of 1943.**

A heavily camouflaged Sdkfz 139 of "Wiking" in Russia.

A "Leibstandarte" Sdkfz 138 in Russia during the winter of 1943/44.

SS-Untersturmführer Claudius Rupp (in 1945 won the German Cross in Gold) with his crew and Sdkfz 138 in Russia, summer 1943 ("Das Reich").

**Effective winter camouflage protects this "Das Reich" Sdkfz 138 in Russia.**

**An Sdkfz 250 of II.SS-Panzer-Korps mounts added firepower in this undated photo.**

Assault guns (Sdkfz 142) of "Das Reich" with Kursk markings on the way to the Russian front in 1943.

This SS/VT Mercedes truck has huge SS runes on the door which can just be seen beside the SS-Untersturmführer in charge.

The Waffen-SS had senior Waffen-SS commanders (Befehlshaber der Waffen-SS) for various non-combat designated areas. Here on the left is SS-Gruppenführer Carl-Maria Demelhuber (Befehlshaber der Waffen-SS Niederlande), Police General Dr. Heinrich Lenkanau, Kriegsmarine Knight's Cross holder and commander of the "Scharnhorst" Kurt Hoffmann, SS-Brigadeführer Dr. Wilhelm Harster and in Diplomatic uniform is SS-Brigadeführer Otto Bene. Note the Dutch SS man in the background with a peaked hat showing their distinctive insignia.

Himmler visits men of the 17.SS-Panzer-Grenadier-Division "Götz von Berlichingen." Here Himmler speaks with regimental commander and Knight's Cross holder SS-Sturmbannführer Jakob Fick. On the far left is the commander of the division, SS-Oberführer Werner Ostendorff. In black panzer uniform is SS-Obergruppenführer Josef "Sepp" Dietrich and beside him the Higher SS and Police Leader for France, SS-Gruppenführer Karl Oberg.

THIS PAGE AND OPPOSITE: Four views of well camouflaged assault guns of the Sturmgeschützbatterie of the SS-Kavallerie-Division in the spring of 1943. The unit had both long and short barrel models.

THIS PAGE AND OPPOSITE: SS-Obersturmbannführer Wolfgang Joerchel (commander SS-Freiwilligen-Panzer-Grenadier-Regiment 48 "General Seyffardt") during and after being awarded the Knight's Cross by SS-Brigadeführer Jürgen Wagner (commander 23.SS-Freiwilligen-Panzer-Grenadier-Division "Nederland").

SS-Obersturmbannführer Max Wüusche presents winter relief funds in the name of I.SS-Panzer-Korps to Hitler and the German people while Heinrich Himmler looks on.

A mid-war photo of SS-Oberführer Fritz von Scholz with SS-Sturmbannführer Walter Plöw. Scholz won the Swords to the Knight's Cross as an SS-Gruppenführer and commander of Division "Nordland" while Plöw was awarded the German Cross in Gold as commander of SS-Flak Abteilung 11 in the same division.

An eight wheeled radio command car of "Germania" during January 1940.

These SS troops and reconnaissance vehicles are at the Spanish border following the western campaign of 1940.

During the early campaigns vehicles were often named in memory of crewmen killed in action. These two armored cars display such memorials after the western campaign with the death date of the crewman also added. The eight wheeled car was the vehicle of Fritz Langanke, later a Panzer Regiment "Das Reich" Knight's Cross holder.

The commander of the SS-Kavallerie-Division in mid-1943, SS-Brigadeführer Hermann Fegelein. Fegelein would win the Swords for this command. On the left is his brother Waldemar Fegelein, a regimental commander in that division and also a Knight's Cross holder.

In Norway an SS designed guard post stands in front of the area commander's residence.

Men of the Army and SS being interviewed by Josef Goebbels. Second from right is later "Wiking" Knight's Cross holder SS-Untersturmführer Werner Meyer.

An autographed photo of "Totenkopf" Knight's Cross holder Josef Rölleke.

**SS-Hauptscharführer Willi Essinger won the Knight's Cross with the anti-tank unit of "Wiking" on June 19, 1943. He was killed on August 25, 1944.**

A "Totenkopf" Division artillery vehicle (note tactical markings and Death's Head emblem) during 1939. Standing on the right is later SS-Standartenführer, divisional commander and German Cross winner Martin Stange.

An anti-tank position during the Mius river fighting in August 1943.

Two views of motorcycle troops of "Das Reich" during the summer 1941 Russian campaign.

**A "Leibstandarte" Sdkfz 251 in Russia.**

**An Sdkfz 251 of an unknown SS unit in Russia.**

A hand made wooden podium with SS runes being used by SS-Obersturmbannführer Hans Kempin, commander of SS-Panzer-Grenadier-Schule Kleinschlag.

An unpublished portrait of Paul Trabandt, Knight's Cross winner with the anti-tank unit of "Wiking."

Mounted rocket projectors used hollow charge rounds and produced high volume fire with very effective results. These two photos show vehicles attached to V.SS-Gebirgs-Korps during the winter of 1944/1945.

A staff car of "Wiking" negotiates Russian marshes (note divisional emblem).

The men on this semi-tracked prime mover gives some indication of the vehicle's size. The large variants could tow tanks though several were needed for heavier types such as the "Tiger."

SS-Sturmbannführer Hans Dorr of "Wiking" being awarded the Swords by Hitler. In the background in white tunic with German Cross is Richard Schulze, later the last commander of SS-Junkerschule "Bad Tölz."

SS-Oberführer Hermann Fegelein with officers of the SS-Kavallerie-Division. Behind him with German Cross is Hans Diergarten (1st Staff Officer and later Knight's Cross winner). The SS-Sturmbannführer is Hermann Gadischke, commander of the division's supply troops.

"Totenkopf" Panzer Regiment "Knight's Cross holder SS-Hauptsturm-führer Waldemar Riefkogel.

SS-Oberführer Felix Steiner as commander of Regiment "Deutschland" during the brief time collar insignia were removed for security reasons. Steiner ended the war as an SS-Obergruppenführer decorated with the Swords to the Knight's Cross and died in 1966.

Otto Kumm was Chief of Staff of V.SS-Gebirgs-Korps when this photo was taken but still wears his "Der Führer" cufftitle from his previous assignment as a regimental commander.

SS-Untersturmführer Otto Weidinger and SS-Obersturmbannführer Dr. Wim Brandt (the inventor of camouflage clothing) decorate reconnaissance troops after the western campaign in 1940. Note the early black panzer berets in use.

A well camouflaged Sdkfz 251 of II.SS-Panzer-Korps during the Normandy campaign.

Use of double SS collar insignia was rare but not as much as some texts believe as seen in this formal portrait of SS-Kavallerie-Division artillery regiment German Cross winner Albert Scheufele.

In the early pre-war period, WWI helmets with new insignia were issued as worn here by SS-Hauptsturmführer Otto Kumm of Regiment "Germania" (note "2" collar insignia for that regiment). Kumm ended the war as an SS-Brigadeführer and Swords to the Knight's Cross holder in command of "Leibstandarte." In the earlier war years he commanded Regiment "Der Führer" and then the 7.SS-Gebirgs-Division "Prinz Eugen." After the war he founded the Waffen-SS veterans group (HIAG) in Hamburg during 1950 and later wrote the official history of "Prinz Eugen."

Full camo jackets are worn with early overseas caps by these engineer troops in 1939-40.

Double "Totenkopf" collar insignia and cufftitle (for "Oberbayern") being worn in 1939 by later German Cross holder and divisional commander Martin Stange.

Note the wire helmet covers to attach additional camouflage on these troops of "Deutschland." The SS-Sturmbannführer is Walter Krüger, later an SS-Obergruppenführer and Swords to the Knight's Cross holder. He was at the time of this photo commander of IV./"Deutschland" (note cufftitle).

A Porsche amphibious vehicle from the reconnaissance detachment staff of "Das Reich."

A Hummel (15cm self-propelled artillery) of "Wiking."

Early assault guns of the assault gun battery added to "Reich" for the 1941 Russian campaign. These were the only armored guns of the division for this campaign and were very effective until the last one was destroyed in January 1942.

Oakleaves winner SS-Sturmbannführer Hans Dorr (later Swords holder) with his adjutant SS-Untersturmführer Günther Jahnke. Jahnke won the German Cross in Gold on February 8, 1945.

Regiment "Der Führer" battalion commander Vincenz Kaiser on top of his semi-tracked command vehicle in Russia. He was killed in April 1945 having won the Knight's Cross with "Der Führer" and the Oakleaves with "Götz von Berlichingen."

A late war winter camouflaged Sdkfz 251 of "Wiking."

From left are Heinrich Himmler, SS-Obergruppenführer Sepp Dietrich and the commander of SS-Panzer-Jäger-Abteilung 17 ("Götz von Berlichingen") SS-Sturmbannführer Friedrich Schuster.

A T-34 captured in Kharkov at the tank factory being inspected by Himmler and, in black uniform, Knight's Cross holder Georg Schönberger (commander of the "Leibstandarte" Panzer Regiment). Between them in profile is Sepp Dietrich. Many of the tanks were repaired and used by Waffen-SS troops until maintenance became impossible.

Two views of the October 13, 1943 funeral in Korssum of Swords to the Knight's Cross holder August Diekmann of "Wiking."

In Holland (1940) Paul Hausser reviews a parade after awarding the Knight's Cross to Fritz Vogt (standing in front of Hausser). Beside Vogt is his reconnaissance detachment commander, SS-Obersturmbannführer Dr. Wim Brandt.

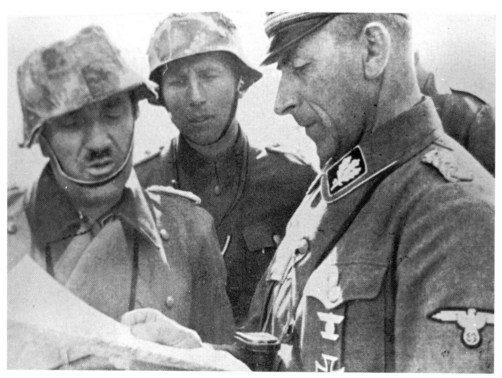

SS-Brigadeführer Paul Hausser with early insignia confers with Carl-Maria Demelhuber (commander of Regiment "Germania") during the 1940 campaign. RIGHT: A signed photo of SS-Standartenführer Ernst Deutsch. In the pre-war period he commanded SS-Bataillon "N" as the youngest SS-Sturmbannführer. Here he is a regimental commander (SS-Gebirgs-Jäger-Regiment 13 "Artur Phleps") with the 7.SS-Gebirgs-Division "Prinz Eugen" where he won the German Cross in Gold on January 7, 1945.

SS-Obersturmführer Rudolf Garscha wears a double breasted camo uniform displaying his decorations including his German Cross in Gold awarded on April 23, 1944. He served with the Artillerie Regiment of "Das Reich."

**SS-Hauptsturmführer Martin Stange instructs early "Totenkopf" recruits in 1939.**

**SS-Brigadeführer Paul Hausser awards the Knight's Cross to SS-Untersturmführer Ludwig Kepplinger of Regiment "Der Führer" in 1940.**

A newly painted assault gun of "Das Reich" in the summer of 1943.

A "Hummel" from the artillery regiment of "Wiking" in Russia during March 1943.

Albert Müller (center) receives the Knight's Cross from "Wiking" divisional commander SS-Brigadeführer Herbert Gille (left) and Manfred Schönfelder (1st Staff Officer). The latter two officers wear white summer issue uniforms.

Later Swords holder and "Wiking" regimental commander Hans Dorr as an enlisted man with "Deutschland" before the war.

Note the uniforms and key symbol in this photo of a "Leibstandarte" reconnaissance car crew. The word "Dietrich" means "key" in German, hence the symbol for Sepp Dietrich, commander of the "LAH."

Two other views of mobile rocket launchers of V.SS-Gebirgs-Korps during the winter of 1944/45.

**OPPOSITE AND ABOVE:** These two photos of SS/VT reconnaissance cars show typical fender unit markings for the late pre-war period.

A variety of cars being used by an SS anti-tank unit (note marking on the nearest vehicle's fender).

THIS PAGE AND OPPOSITE: These five photos show Josef Lainer (Regiment "Der Führer") being awarded the Knight's Cross by "Das Reich" commander Walter Krüger and Regiment "Der Führer" commander Sylvester Stadler in 1943. In the last photo both Lainer and Krüger review the troops after the award has been made.

**SS-Oberführer Paul Hausser (center) during a tour of SS-Junkerschule Braunschweig in 1936.**

**In 1943 an SS self-propelled anti-tank gun moves towards the front with gun covered for road travel.**

Two views of the anti-tank weapon of Erich Rossner, the only Knight's Cross holder of the "Das Reich" anti-tank unit. His award decorates the guard of the weapon and the barrel shows the number of enemy vehicles destroyed.

LEFT: SS-Obersturmführer Karl Nikolussi-Leck, awarded the Knight's Cross as commander of 8th Company, SS-Panzer-Regiment 5 "Wiking" on April 9, 1944. RIGHT: II.SS-Panzer-Korps officers in Russia during 1943. On the right is Chief of Staff Werner Ostendorf (later commander of "Götz von Berlichingen" and "Das Reich" as well as an Oakleaves holder), Paul Hausser and on the far left in black Panzer uniform is Hans-Albin von Reitzenstein (Knight's Cross as commander of the "Das Reich" Panzer Regiment).

Early Waffen-SS anti-tank troops in training (note low silhouette of the weapon).

**A prime mover towing an anti-tank gun of II.SS-Panzer-Korps in the summer of 1942.**

**SS-Brigadeführer Hermann Fegelein (commander SS-Kavallerie-Division) and Hans Diergarten (Ia) during the summer of 1943.**

Four of the many important commanders in "Leibstandarte," three of whom won the Knight's Cross with Oakleaves or higher. From left are Fritz Witt, Josef "Sepp" Dietrich, Walter Staudinger (artillery regiment commander) and Theodor Wisch.

Heinz Harmel ("Deutschland") being awarded the Oakleaves by Hitler while Otto Baum ("Totenkopf") waits to be given the same decoration. Reichsführer-SS Heinrich Himmler observes at right.

SS-Obergruppenführer Sepp Dietrich in black Panzer uniform showing his Swords to the Knight's Cross.

This early "Totenkopf" column shows the variety of Death's Head emblems used. Two different styles are on the lead motorcycle.

Men of the SS Wallonie unit led by Leon Degrelle take their oath. Note the sleeve shields and cufftitles.

A Panzer IV and an assault gun of "Das Reich" during the Normandy campaign.

The ceremony activating the 17.SS-Panzer-Grenadier-Division "Götz von Berlichingen" in April 1944. Note the divisional emblem above the stage.

Leaving the "Götz von Berlichingen" activation ceremony are, from left, SS-Obergruppenführer Sepp Dietrich, SS-Oberführer Werner Ostendorf and Heinrich Himmler.

**Autographed photo of SS-Sturmbannführer Otto Baum. Baum won his German Cross, Knight's Cross and Oakleaves to the Knight's Cross with "Totenkopf" commanding a battalion and later a regiment. As commander of "Das Reich" he won the Swords and ended the war as an SS-Oberführer in command of the 16.SS-Panzer-Grenadier-Division "Reichsführer-SS."**

Sepp Dietrich, Heinrich Himmler and Karl Oberg (Higher SS and Police Leader) take a pause during a 1944 trip. Note command flags on the cars of their column.

Heinz Harmel (commander Regiment "Deutschland") visits an SS cemetery in Russia.

Otto Kumm (left) the commander of Regiment "Der Führer" and Vincenz Kaiser (battalion commander "Der Führer") in 1943. Note Kaiser's single handed tank destruction sleeve strips.

Three Knight's Cross holders of "Deutschland" in full camo. From left are Helmut Schreiber, Heinz Harmel and Günther Wisliceny. Wisliceny became the last commander of "Deutschland" and won the Swords as did Harmel who ended the war as an SS-Brigadeführer commanding the 10.SS-Panzer-Division "Frundsberg."

A signed photo of SS-Polizei-Division Knight's Cross holder Hans Traupe.

Hugo Eichhorn (left) who won the Knight's Cross in command of the "Wiking" Engineer Battalion is shown here with his adjutant when commanding the SS Engineer Training and Replacement unit in Dresden.

**RIGHT:**
The commander of the 1.SS-Infanterie-Brigade (mot) SS-Standartenführer August-Wilhelm Trabandt (left) and SS-Hauptsturmführer Ernst Schäfer. Trabandt ended the war an SS-Brigadeführer.

A "Leibstandarte" radio command vehicle in Russia during 1941. Himmler (middle) talks with Sepp Dietrich while Georg Schönberger in black panzer uniform looks on. Photo taken in Kharkov during 1943.

SS-Oberführer Werner Ostendorf (right) speaks to Hermann Buch during activation of "Götz von Berlichingen." Between them is "Leibstandarte" Knight's Cross holder Hermann Weiser.

In these two photos Hitler, Himmler and Karl Wolff (Himmler's adjutant) inspect an SS guard of honor commanded by a police officer.

SS-Obergruppenführer Artur Phleps with his staff. Phleps commanded "Prinz Eugen" and later the V.SS-Gebirgs-Korps. He is shown wearing his Knight's Cross won for his divisional command.

At Hitler's headquarters are from left Max Wünsche, Sepp Dietrich, Hitler, Theodor Wisch, Fritz Witt and Otto Günsche.

Himmler visits "Wiking" and walks with SS-Brigadeführer Herbert Gille (divisional commander and Diamonds winner) and August Diekmann (regimental commander and Swords winner).

Himmler (2nd from left) and Kurt Daleuge (Order Police commander) with two new Knight's Cross holders of the SS-Polizei-Division. On the far left is Bernhard Griese and second from right is Rudolf Pannier.

An autographed photo of Regiment "Deutschland" commander Günther Wisliceny.

SS-Sturmbannführer Christian Tychsen, commander of the "Das Reich" Panzer Regiment. As an SS-Obersturmbannführer and Oakleaves winner he was killed in the Normandy campaign commanding "Das Reich."

SS-Sturmbannführer Gerd Bremer (note "LAH" shoulder monogram).

**Willi Hein, later a company commander and Knight's Cross holder with Panzer Regiment "Wiking," is shown in an early pre-war signed photo.**

RIGHT: SS-Obergruppenführer Artur Phleps, SS-Standartenführer Otto Kumm and SS-Sturmbannführer Hans Kempin during a visit to the SS-Panzer-Grenadier school.

BELOW: SS-Gruppenführer Artur Phleps as commander of "Prinz Eugen."

Erwin Meierdress being awarded the Oakleaves by Hitler, 1943.

Otto Weidinger's company of Regiment "Deutschland" in 1938. Weidinger later won the Swords and was last commander of Regiment "Der Führer."

A pre-war sporting competition (note the SS sports clothing) with a bronze bust of Hitler being 1st prize.

**Assault guns readied for transport, "Das Reich" 1943.**

**A destroyed assault gun of "Das Reich" in Russia, summer 1943.**

ABOVE AND BELOW: Both of these SS-Obersturmführer won the German Cross in Gold with one of the foreign volunteer divisions. Any help with naming these men would be appreciated.

SS-Sturmbannführer Matthias Kleinheisterkamp wears the "B" collar tab and his dress SS dagger while instructing at Braunschweig in this pre-war photo. He ended the war as a corps commander and Oakleaves winner.

The commander of "Wiking" Felix Steiner (right) in 1941 with his reconnaissance detachment commander Hans-Albin von Reitzenstein (later Knight's Cross holder with "Das Reich").

SS-Obersturmführer Rudolf Enseling of the SS/VT Engineer Battalion wearing a cufftitle and special collar insignia for that unit. He won the German Cross in Gold with the Engineer Battalion of "Das Reich" and the Knight's Cross as an SS-Sturmbannführer in command of that division's Tank Regiment, ending the war as an SS-Obersturmbannführer.

MG-34s on a half track serve as anti-aircraft defense in this February 1942 photo.

Paul Hausser lectures officers of the SS/VT artillery regiment in mid-1939.

This photo shows the grey assault gun uniforms issued to Sturmgeschütz crews (Russia 1943).

Note the sleeve shield and SS runes on the breast (denoting full time SS officer) of the engineer battailon commander of the 13.Freiwilligen-Gebirgs-Division "Handschar."

Rudolf Sandig, Knight's Cross holder with "Leibstandarte" in Russia.

The mounted kettle drummer of the SS-Kavallerie-Division in 1942.

"Ziethen," an assault gun issued to "Reich" in 1941 as part of the single battery equipped with these weapons.

A radio command armored car of "Totenkopf" in Russia during 1941.

"Leibstandarte" Knight's Cross holder SS-Oberscharführer Kurt Sametreiter.

The SS-Kavallerie-Division in 1943. From left are SS-Obersturmbannführer Günther Temme, SS-Brigadeführer Hermann Fegelein and SS-Standartenführer Gustav Lombard.

SS-Obersturmbannführer Karl Ullrich of "Totenkopf." He led the "Theodor Eicke" regiment at this time and ended the war in command of the 5.SS-Panzer-Division "Wiking" as an SS-Oberführer and Oakleaves winner.

SS-Standartenführer Ernst Ludwig, the commander of SS-Gebirgs-Artillerie-Regiment 7 ("Prinz Eugen") and later the SS artillery training and replacement regiment. Note his mountain sleeve insignia and the "Prinz Eugen" cufftitle on the SS-Sturmbannführer near him.

From the right are SS-Sturmbannführer Kurt Meyer (with Knight's Cross), SS-Hauptsturmführer Max Wünsche and Sepp Dietrich (note early rank insignia) decorating men of "Leibstandarte" in 1941.

Wolfgang Willrich designed art portraits of some Knight's Cross holders in either partial color or black and white. This example, with color facial area, is of "Der Führer" Knight's Cross holder Georg Keppler. He held more senior commands than any other commander and was one of the best Waffen-SS senior commanders.

Officers of "Handschar" wearing their unique Fez and arm shields. The two nearest officers are full time SS members as seen by the Siegrunen below their breast pocket.

Oakleaves winner SS-Brigadeführer Jurgen Wagner (left) commander of Brigade "Nederland" with his Ia, SS-Sturmbannführer Herbert Wienczek.

SS-Oberführer Theodor Wisch (left) with SS-Sturmbannführer Joachim Peiper, both later Swords holders with "Leibstandarte," in Russia.

A promotion ceremony for Max Wünsche of "Hitlerjugend." From left are Kurt Meyer (Swords holder), Wünsche, Sepp Dietrich, Heinrich Himmler and in the background with German Cross in Gold is Hubert Meyer (Ia of the division). Meyer wrote the official history of "Hitlerjugend."

Heinrich Himmler during a visit to "Wiking" rides with divisional commander Felix Steiner (seated behind the driver).

Two photos of Knight's Cross holder Ludwig Kepplinger. As an NCO with "Der Führer" and as a Sturmbannführer and regimental commander with "Götz von Berlichingen" after award of the German Cross in Gold. He was killed on August 6, 1944.

Commanders of the "Leibstandarte" shown from right are SS-Obersturmbannführer Max Wünsche (Oakleaves), SS-Brigadeführer Theodor Wisch (Swords), SS-Obergruppenführer Sepp Dietrich (Diamonds), SS-Oberführer Fritz Witt (Oakleaves) and Otto Günsche (Hitler's SS adjutant).

**THIS PAGE AND OPPOSITE: Paul Hausser, the most admired of all Waffen-SS commanders, gives personal instruction to infantry trainees in these four photos. No doubt a memorable day for the recruits.**

Himmler observing troops of "Wiking." On the right is Swords holder August Dieckmann, then an SS-Sturmbannführer wearing the Knight's Cross.

SS-Standartenführer August-Wilhelm Trabandt reviews men of the 1.SS-Infanterie-Brigade (mot).

OPPOSITE ABOVE: From left are Herbert Gille ("Wiking" commander and Diamonds winner), Heinrich Himmler, and Leon Degrelle (Oakleaves winner). Not Degrelle's sleeve shield. OPPOSITE BELOW: SS-Sturmbannführer Peter Hansen (with binoculars) the commander of the SS/VT artillery regiment observes training with Paul Hausser (to the left of Hansen) during the summer of 1939.

A perfect pose for a modeler. An assault gun of "Das Reich" in Russia, 1943.

A multiple 2cm anti-aircraft gun of II.SS-Panzer-Korps in Russia, winter 1942/43.

Hans Mühlencamp (Oakleaves) congratulates Knight's Cross holder Willi Hein in October 1944. Next to him in this "Wiking" dedicated photo is Knight's Cross holder Kurt Saumenicht.

THIS PAGE AND OPPOSITE: Self propelled anti-tank guns allowed the use of outdated tank types and were very effective. These four views are of vehicles belonging to the Panzerjäger Abteilung of "Das Reich" in 1943.

**ABOVE AND OPPOSITE: Knight's Cross holder Rudolf Sandig in the field with "Leibstandarte."**

**SS-Polizei-Division Knight's Cross holders Bernhard Griese and Rudolf Pannier on the day they were given their decorations by Himmler.**

SS-Sturmbannführer Otto Weidinger with the Knight's Cross won for leadership of the "Das Reich" reconnaissance detachment. He later won the Swords and commanded Regiment "Der Führer."

German Cross holder Sepp Thaler in an early portrait with the rare black Panzer beret.

Joachim Peiper before the war with "Leibstandarte." He was one of the best "LAH" regimental commanders and a Swords to the Knight's Cross holder.

One of the few Wolfgang Willrich art cards of a Waffen-SS Knight's Cross holder. This example shows Fritz Vogt.

ABOVE AND BELOW: Two views of divisional commander Paul Hausser with Fritz Vogt on August 22, 1940: the day Vogt received his Knight's Cross.

**Joachim Peiper being awarded the Swords to the Knight's Cross by Hitler.**

Pre-war engineer officers Heinz Lammerding (right with early model sword) and in the center Max Seela. Both men were awarded the Knight's Cross, Seela with "Totenkopf" and Lammerding with "Das Reich."

ABOVE LEFT: Later Oakleaves to the Knight's Cross and Gold Close Combat Clasp winner Heinz Macher as an enlisted man with the SS/VT engineer battalion (note early style helmet). He ended the war an SS-Sturmbannführer.

ABOVE RIGHT: Leon Degrelle (Oakleaves winner) here as commander of the Brigade "Wallonie" with Knight's Cross in camo uniform.

RIGHT: The pre-war uniform of the SS/VT Pionier (engineers) being worn by later "Leibstandarte" German Cross in Gold winner Ferdinand Fellhauer.

**SS-Oberführer Otto Baum wearing the Swords to the Knight's Cross won during the Normandy campaign. He is shown in Italy as commander of the 16.SS-Panzer-Grenadier-Division "Reichsführer-SS."**

**A small caliber field gun being towed by a car of "Das Reich."**

**Heinz Macher being awarded the Knight's Cross by Hans Jüttner and a signed photo of Macher with the decoration as an SS-Obersturmführer.**

**Anti-tank gunners with camp jackets and helmet covers on the offensive.**

Knight's Cross winner Franz Grohmann in an early portrait as an EM (above) and later as an SS-Obersturmführer with Knight's Cross (below).

Oakleaves winner SS-Obersturmbannführer Christian Tychsen (right) with Knight's Cross holder Dieter Kesten during 1944. Tychsen was killed in Normandy commanding "Das Reich."

**Knight's Cross winner Hans Siegel ("Hitlerjugend") in an early portrait with 15.SS-Totenkopfstandarte (note collar insignia).**

**Dr. Wolfgang Röhder, Knight's Cross holder and assault gun detachment commander.**

"Prinz Eugen" commander SS-Brigadeführer Carl Ritter von Oberkamp (middle) and on the right with Oakleaves is the Chief of Staff for V.SS-Gebirgs-Korps, SS-Standartenführer Otto Kumm.

In Russia during the spring of 1943 are from right Jakob Fick (Knight's Cross), Paul Hausser (Swords), Heinrich Himmler and Walter Krüger (Swords).

"Leibstandarte" Swords holder Joachim Peiper (left) and Heinz von Westernhagen. Westernhagen commanded the "LAH" assault gun unit and later sSS-Panzer-Abteilung 501.

"LAH" Knight's Cross holder SS-Untersturm-führer Werner Wolff after receiving the award. Note his "LAH" shoulder boards.

SS-Obersturmführer Gerd Bremer wears the summer white tunic and displays his Knight's Cross won with "Leibstandarte." He was later awarded the Oakleaves with "Hitlerjugend" as commander of that division's reconnaissance unit.

ABOVE LEFT: Hans Mühlenkamp, the much decorated armored commander of "Wiking" and later a divisional commander.

ABOVE RIGHT: Hermann Fegelein (Swords winner) in Russia during 1943 while commanding the SS-Kavallerie-Division. Note the white summer tunic.

LEFT: Note the skull fender marking on the "Totenkopf" car assigned to the artillery regiment.

Christian Tychsen being awarded the Oakleaves by Hitler. In the background is Knight's Cross holder Fritz Darges.

ABOVE LEFT: A signed portrait of Alois Weber, Knight's Cross holder with "Deutschland."

ABOVE RIGHT: Walter Schmidt being awarded the Knight's Cross by Herbert Gille ("Wiking").

LEFT: In fur hat is Knight's Cross holder Fritz Darges ("Wiking"). Note the Sdkfz 251 with anti-tank gun mounted in the background.

BELOW: "LAH" Knight's Cross holder Rudolf Sandig.

RIGHT: Swords winner SS-Gruppenführer Felix Steiner (right) with Heinrich Himmler.

SS-Standartenführer Hans Mühlenkamp and another KC holder of "Wiking" inspect the vehicle repair unit.

SS-Totenkopfstandarte "Oberbayern" in a pre-war parade led by Knight's Cross holder Kurt Launer. Note the dress uniforms.

ABOVE: A "Totenkopf" motorcycle rider naps in the side car. Note the skull marked rear of the cycle.

RIGHT: Shown as an enlisted man in the SS/VT is later SS-Obersturm-bannführer and Swords holder Günther Wisliceny. He was the last commander of "Deutschland."

BELOW: Three Knight's Cross holders during a speaking tour. From right are Heinz Macher, Waldemar Riefkogel and Ludwig Kepplinger.

Otto Weidinger (last commander "Der Führer") being honored on the day he won the Knight's Cross.

An unpublished signed portrait of Knight's Cross holder Hans Scherg.

Hugo Eichhorn, Knight's Cross holder with the Engineer Battalion of "Wiking."

The assault gun tunic (note "P" for Panzerjäger shoulder monogram) and German Cross in cloth version being worn by eventual Oakleaves winner Ernst August Krag.

An armored car of "Das Reich" in the summer of 1941 (note emblem on front of the vehicle).

Troops man-handle an infantry gun through the Russian mud in the spring of 1942

A good view of the "Totenkopf" enlisted man's uniform of later German Cross in Gold holder Johann Bosch.

**SS-Oberführer Walter Staudinger, "Leibstandarte" artillery commander, wearing a variety of foreign awards in addition to his German Cross in Gold.**

Panzer Regiment 5 detachment commander and Knight's Cross holder Willi Hein congratulates newly decorated armored troops of "Wiking."

"Totenkopf" commander Theodor Eicke celebrates his award of the Oakleaves with Feldmarschal Wilhelm Keitel. On the left is Himmler's adjutant Karl Wolff.

A celebration of the staff of "Horst Wessel" with divisional commander SS-Standartenführer August-Wilhelm Trabandt and new Knight's Cross holder Heinrich Sonne, motorcycle company commander of the reconnaissance detachment.

"Wiking" regimental commander Hans Dorr being presented with the Oakleaves while divisional commander waits to be awarded the same decoration.

**Dr. Joseph Goebbels with Knight's Cross holders (from right) Heinz Macher, Hermann Buchner, Hugo Kraas, Max Wünsche and Kurt Meyer.**

**In the center of this group during the formation of "Totenkopf" Division is commander Theodor Eicke.**

An assault gun of the single battery attached to "Reich" during the funeral of an officer.

Troops man-handle their anti-tank gun into position in Russia.

**Shown in early style uniforms, these SS/VT officers and men were attached to the Pioniersturmbann (engineer battalion).**

**A prime mover of the anti-tank detachment of "Das Reich" passes through a burning Russian village.**

The semi-tracked Sdkfz 250 and 251 were the workhorses of the Panzergrenadier units. These two views are from II.SS-Panzer-Korps in Russia.

Note the collar insignia on "Prinz Eugen" officer Otto Bayer. On the right with Oakleaves is Otto Kumm (Chief of Staff, V.SS-Gebirgs-Korps) and in the rear is "Prinz Eugen" commander Carl von Oberkamp.

The commander of II.SS-Panzer-Korps, SS-Obergruppenführer Paul Hausser (right), lunches with the staff of "Das Reich."

**A Waffen-SS Tiger in France during the Normandy campaign.**

**Pzkpfw IV number 813 in France, 1944.**

A view showing unloading of assault guns for II.SS-Panzer-Korps in Russia, 1943.

Early short barreled assault guns of "Reich" in 1941.

Two Panther photos. Though often unmarked, the upper one is "Das Reich" and the lower view is from "Wiking."

Himmler inspects early SS/VT troops from "Deutschland." Note the early "D" shoulder insignia and overseas caps.

The commander and senior staff of "Der Führer" regiment confer in Vienna, 1945. Note the staff marked car.

**II.SS-Panzer-Korps assault guns being transported and readied in Russia, 1943.**

**A Tiger during the Normandy campaign.**

**Panzergrenadiers take a welcome ride on a Sdkfz 250 in Russia, 1943.**

A 1936 photo of an SS/VT band showing their unique shoulder insignia and early helmets.

## AUTHOR'S REQUEST

The creation of this volume and previous books has been possible with the help of numerous individuals. Research continues on a variety of SS related themes and further material is needed in response to reader requests for subject topics. Particularly sought are photographs of any personalities (especially German Cross holders), ceremonies and weapons. Books and periodicals related to the SS and tangent topics are sought as well. Photocopies of award documents (all types) are also particularly needed. Readers wishing to loan, trade or sell material for use in future volumes are asked to contact the author. Materials used will be credited and a copy of the volume containing the material will be provided to the contributor by the author. Correspondence with other historians, researchers and authors for the exchange of material is welcome.

Mark C. Yerger
P.O. Box 4485
Lancaster, PA 17604
U.S.A.

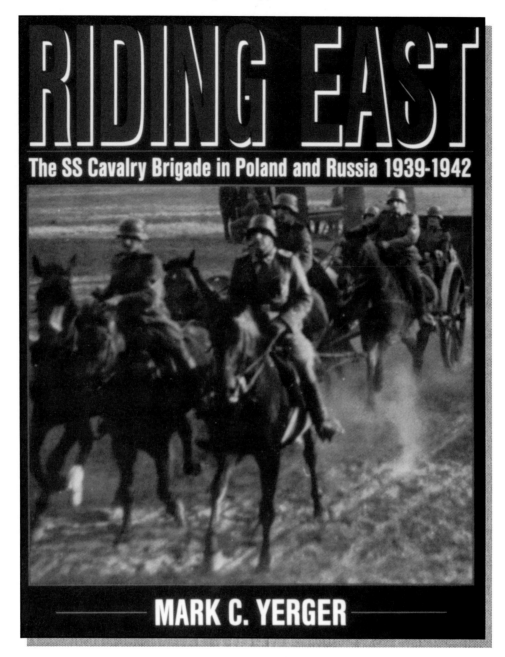

# RIDING EAST
## THE SS CAVALRY BRIGADE IN POLAND AND RUSSIA
### 1939-1942
### Mark C. Yerger

RIDING EAST details the history of the previously unexamined SS Cavalry Brigade. Beginning with a background of the General SS mounted units, from which personnel formed part of the Brigade's cadre, the author details the organization, units and commanders of these pre-war formations. A detailed biography of Hermann Fegelein, commander of the Brigade, is followed by a chapter devoted to the SS command in Poland where the Brigade operated during 1939-40 as an occupational force. The units themselves are next examined from first creation in 1939 until they divided into two regiments in 1941, including all duties and operations in Poland. Assigned to the Headquarters Staff "Reichsführer-SS" at the start of the invasion of Russia, the regiments then combined with other units to form the SS-Cavalry Brigade and conducted anti-partisan warfare operations for most of the remainder of 1941. All the summer 1941 operations are examined in depth, including the massive Pripet marshes actions, using original documents from American and European archive sources. Subordinated in 1942 to Army Group "Center," the SS-Cavalry Brigade fought at the front during the massive Russian offensive in 1942 and was almost completely annihilated in the Rshev area before finally being withdrawn and used as cadre for the new SS-Kavallerie-Division. Heavily documented, the detailed text is supplemented by 109 photographs, most of which are previously unpublished. In addition, six maps, six Order of Battle charts, complete officer rosters 1939-1942, Feldpost numbers, details of primary commanders within the Brigade, as well information on the units and commanders it was subordinated to, complete a comprehensive history of the first combat mounted unit of the SS.

Size: 8 1/2" x 11"   224 pages      b/w photographs, documents
ISBN: 0-7643-0060-1        hard cover            $59.95